GENETIC ANCESTRY TESTING

HEREDITY AND GENETICS

GENETIC ANCESTRY TESTING

Kristi Lew

Enslow Publishing
101 W. 23rd Street
Suite 240
New York, NY 10011
USA
enslow.com

Published in 2019 by Enslow Publishing, LLC
101 W. 23rd Street, Suite 240, New York, NY 10011

Cataloging-in-Publication Data

Names: Lew, Kristi.
Title: Genetic ancestry testing / Kristi Lew.
Description: New York : Enslow Publishing, 2019. | Series: Heredity and genetics | Includes bibliographic references and index. | Audience: Grades 7-12.
Identifiers: ISBN 9780766099487 (pbk.) | ISBN 9780766099470 (library bound)
Subjects: LCSH: Genetics—Juvenile literature. | Genetic genealogy—Juvenile literature.
Classification: LCC QH437.5 L49 2019 | DDC 572.8—dc23

Printed in the United States of America

To Our Readers: We have done our best to make sure all websites in this book were active and appropriate when we went to press. However, the author and the publisher have no control over and assume no liability for the material available on those websites or on any websites they may link to. Any comments or suggestions can be sent by email to customerservice@enslow.com.

Photo credits: Cover, p. 1 Andrew Brookes/Cultura/Getty Images; p. 6 Sarah Weldon FRGS/Shutterstock.com; p. 8 Mario Villafuerte/Getty Images; p. 11 Tefi/Shutterstock.com; p. 12 Zvitaliy/Shutterstock.com; p. 14 Alfred Pasieka/Science Photo Library/Getty Images; p. 18 NYPL/Science Source/Getty Images; p. 21 Hulton Archive/Archive Photos/Getty Images; p. 23 Designua/Shutterstock.com; p. 26 Tek Image/Science Photo Library/Science Photo Library/Getty Images; p. 28 Science Stock Photography/Science Source; pp. 32–33 BSIP/Universal Images Group/Getty Images; p. 35 Sakurra/Shutterstock.com; p. 39 Everett Historical/Shutterstock.com; p. 43 Christian Jegou Publiphoto Diffusion/Science Source; p. 44 Izzet Keribar/Lonely Planet Images/Getty Images; p. 48 Claus Lunau/Science Source; p. 52 Tetiana Iatsenko/Shutterstock.com; p. 54 Africa Studio/Shutterstock.com; p. 57 coxy58/Shutterstock.com; p. 59 Francis DeMange/Gamma-Rapho/Getty Images; p. 62 Biophoto Associates/Science Source; p. 64 National Institute on Aging/NIH/Science Source; p. 66 AF archive/Alamy Stock Photo; p. 68 Kirn Vintage Stock/Corbis Historical; interior page headers Juli Hansen/Shutterstock.com (DNA strand); interior page backgrounds and back cover paulista/Shutterstock.com (DNA double helix).

Contents

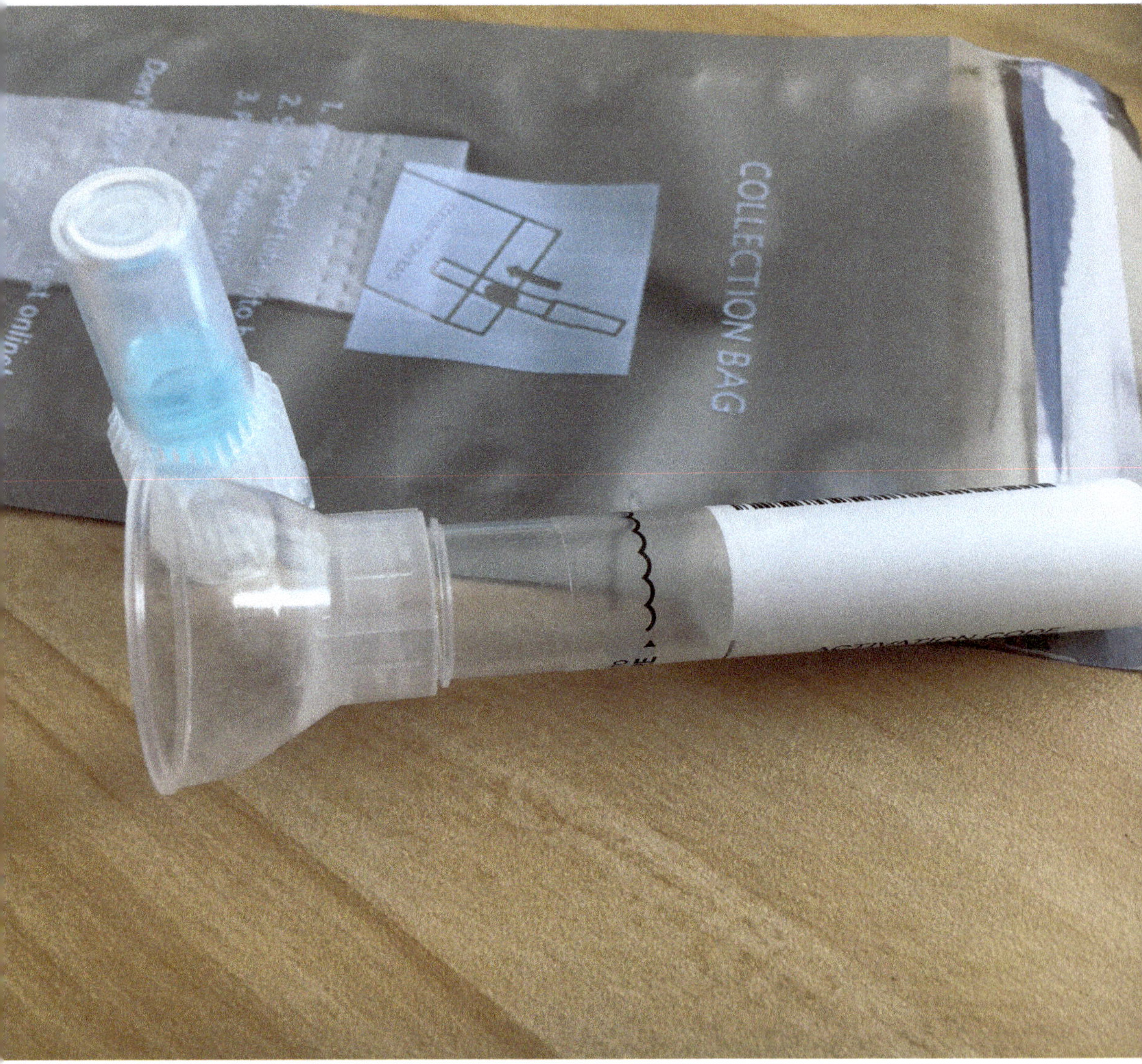

Some genetic genealogy test kits require test takers to fill a tube with saliva. DNA is extracted from sloughed off cheek cells contained within the saliva sample.

Introduction

Where did I come from? How do I fit in? These two questions are some of the most fundamental questions in all of humanity. Looking for a sense of belonging often leads people to peer into their pasts. Understanding the cultures, traditions, and choices made by their ancestors can sometimes help people understand themselves better. This need for a connection may account for how genealogy, or the tracing of ancestral lines, has become the second most popular hobby in the United States, according to *Time* magazine.

Genealogists have long searched for answers in legal documents, church records, and photographs. In an attempt to fit the pieces of a family history together, a genealogist looks for links in birth, marriage, divorce, and death certificates as well as census and immigration documents. Sometimes these attempts are thwarted by incomplete records, which may be caused by adoption, social strife, or family secrets.

Now, genealogy has entered a new age. One in which long-lost, distant relatives are an internet search away and a person's DNA, or at least part of it, can be analyzed for answers that documents cannot reveal. A proliferation of profitable genealogy websites, popular television shows, and newly published books have been

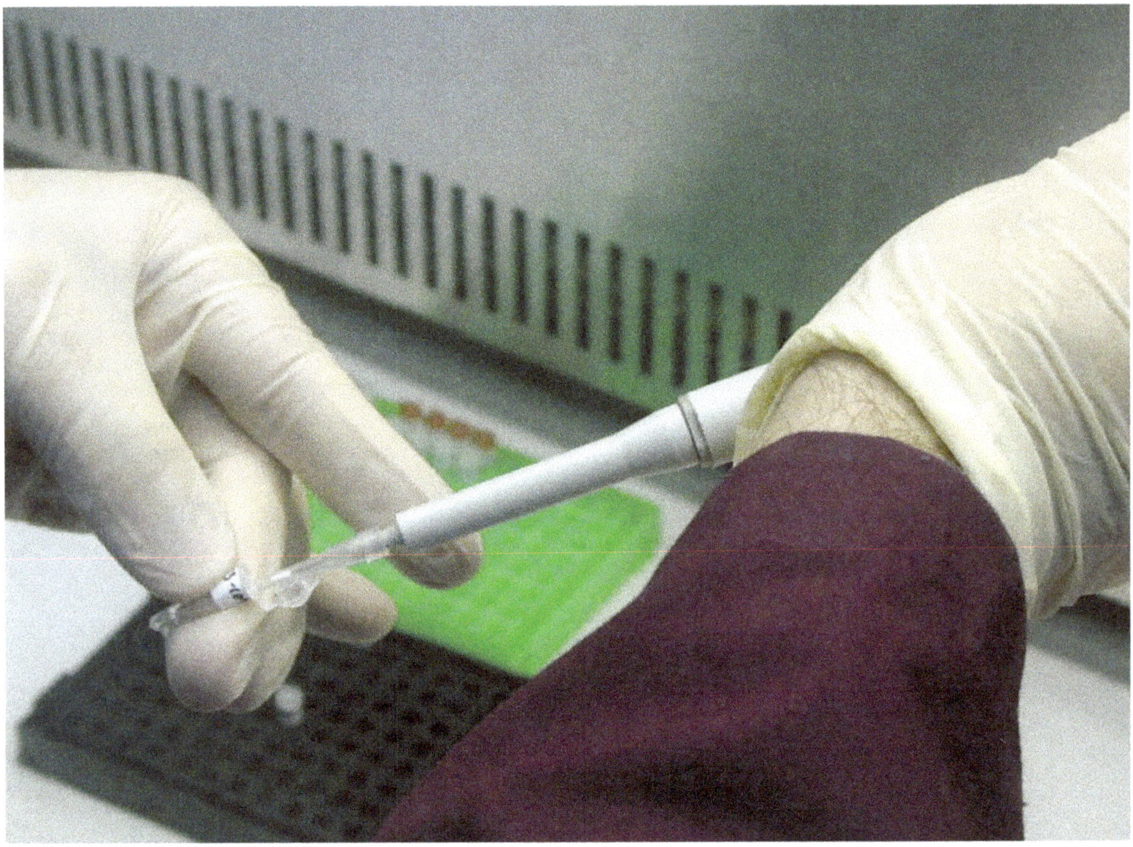

A forensic analyst prepares a sample for DNA sequencing. DNA from different crime scenes and suspects can then be compared for matching genetic markers.

produced to feed the public's fascination with finding their roots. They have also transformed the genealogy industry into a billion dollar business.

With the advent of over-the-counter genetic testing kits in the early 2000s and the DNA databases that have sprung up around them, anyone interested in their family's history can now quickly, easily, and inexpensively discover kin they never knew existed. All they have to do is swab the inside of their cheek to gather a few skin cells and send the sample off to a genetic genealogy company. In return, test takers receive a report listing all the people in the company's databases that have similar stretches of DNA, indicating they may be related.

DNA sequencing, or fingerprinting, was first developed to assist geneticists, criminologists, and historians. The technology was used to determine if changes in the DNA sequence caused specific diseases, if DNA left behind at a crime scene matched a suspect's DNA, or if the bones found in a grave belong to a particular person or family. Since then, genealogists and anthropologists have appropriated DNA sequencing to help inform the study of human history on a larger scale.

Together, the internet and DNA testing have revolutionized not only the pursuit of a single family's history but the ancient roots of the larger human family as well. What was once a largely solitary pursuit requiring day-long trips to far-flung records offices and weeks-long correspondence through the mail has turned into the online research of digitized records and group-sourced DNA databases.

Discovering the identities of ancestors can bring with it emotional and intellectual rewards. However, it can also bring about circumstances that were not considered before undertaking the reconstruction of genetic and genealogical family trees. An understanding of how genetic genealogy works, what types of relationships it can—and cannot—reveal, and how it might affect individual privacy may help avert some unintended consequences and allow ancestral research and discovery with minimal disruption to contemporary familial relationships.

1

Understanding Inheritance

To understand how genetic genealogy works and how it can and cannot reveal family relationships, it is helpful to know how genetic material is passed from generation to generation.

DNA and Heredity

Genetic information is stored in a long, complex molecule called deoxyribonucleic acid, or DNA. Most DNA resides in the nucleus of a cell, but a small amount can also be found in the mitochondria. Mitochondria are tiny organelles in the cell's cytoplasm that convert the nutrients in food into energy that the cell can use to carry out its functions. For this reason, biologists often call mitochondrion the powerhouse of the cell. Cells may have hundreds or thousands of mitochondria.

The shape of the DNA molecule can be compared to a twisted ladder. This type of structure is called a double helix. The sides of the ladder are made up of phosphate and sugar molecules. The rungs are made up of pairs of nitrogen bases. There are four types of nitrogen bases—adenine (A), cytosine (C), guanine (G), and thymine (T)—and they pair with one another in a very specific

ANATOMY OF A CELL

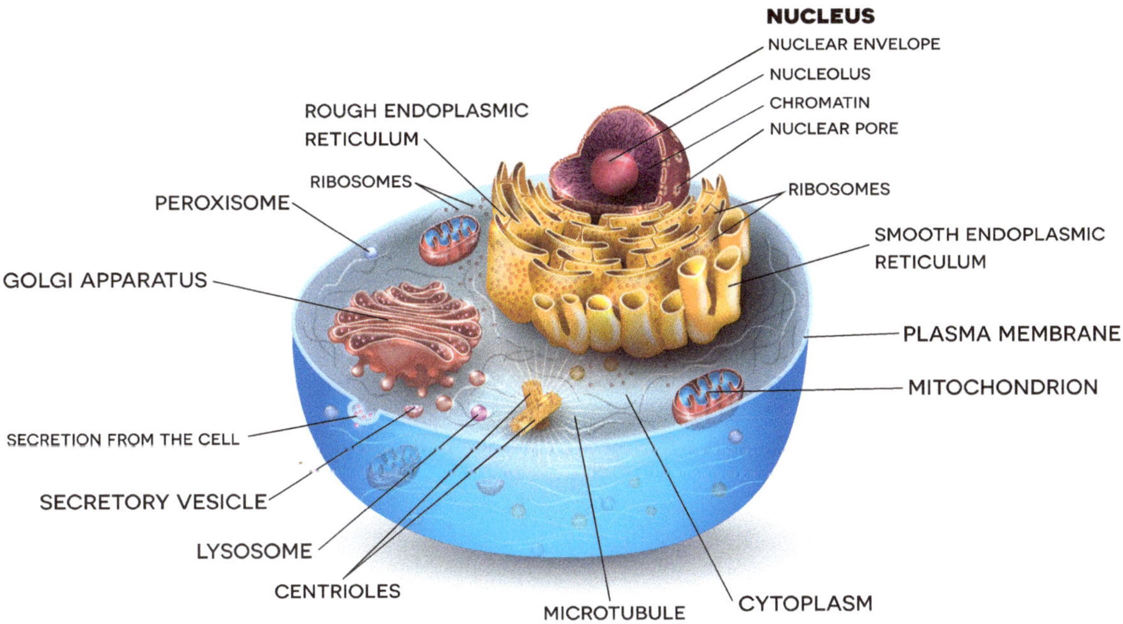

A majority of the DNA that makes up the human genome is found in the nucleus of the cell. The rest can be found in the mitochondria.

DNA double helix

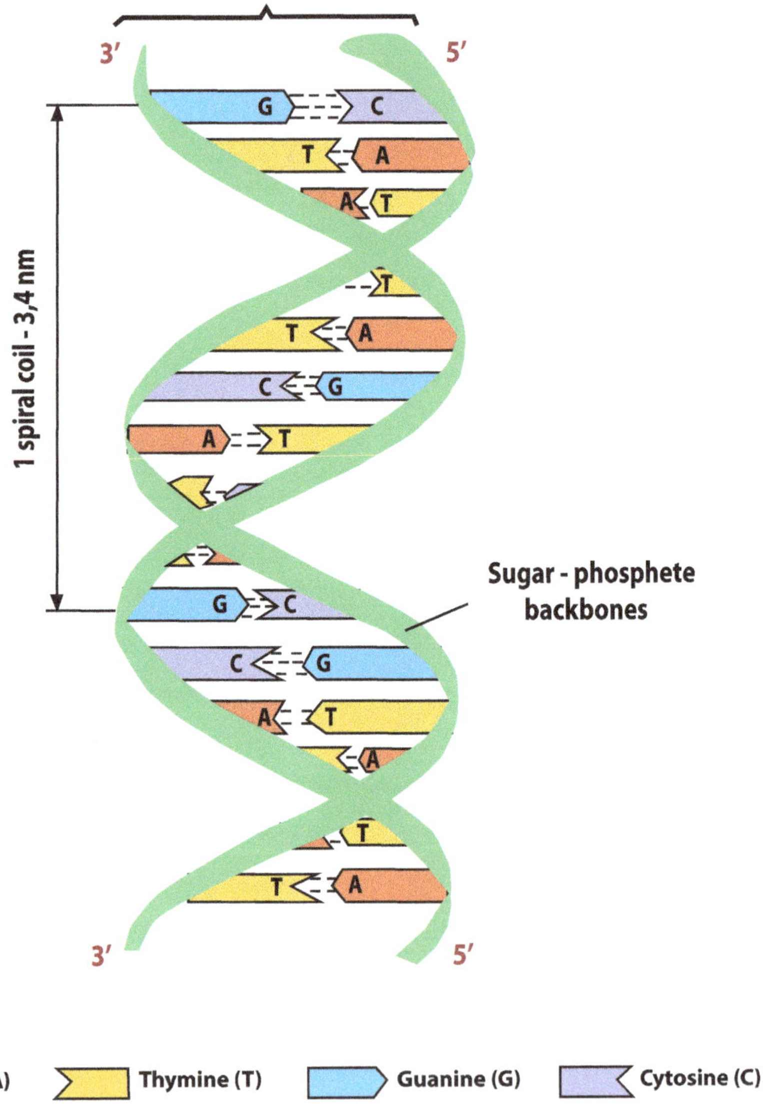

The four nitrogen bases in a DNA molecule pair off in a predictable manner. During cell division, strands of DNA are replicated, or copied. Mistakes made during this copying process can be traced from generation to generation.

way. Adenine always pairs with thymine. And cytosine is always paired with guanine.

Because of the way DNA bases pair with one another, one strand of DNA serves as a pattern for duplicating the other strand. When a cell divides, an exact copy of the DNA present in the parent cell is replicated. Occasionally, however, mistakes are made during this copying process. These mistakes are called mutations. Most mutations are benign, meaning they have no effect on the person who inherits them. These differences in base pair order can be passed down to the next generation and scientists can use them to trace ancestry back through time.

An organism's complete set of DNA—both nuclear and mitochondrial—is called its genome. An organism's genome contains all the information needed to build, maintain, and repair that organism. Along the DNA molecule, specific sequences of base pairs tell the cell how to make particular proteins. Each protein is specialized to carry out a unique function in the organism. These specific base sequences are called genes. Genes can range in size from a few hundred bases to more than two million.

The human genome is remarkably similar from person to person. Nearly all genes are exactly the same in most people. However, a small amount, around one percent, is slightly different. One percent of the human genome means that only about one in one thousand bases differ between individuals. Forms of the same gene that have slight differences in DNA sequence are called alleles. The slight differences in alleles contribute to each person's unique physical features.

Nuclear DNA is packaged into forty-six structures called chromosomes. Chromosomes consist of strands of DNA wrapped around proteins called histones. Most human cells contain twenty-three pairs of chromosomes. Twenty-two of these chromosome

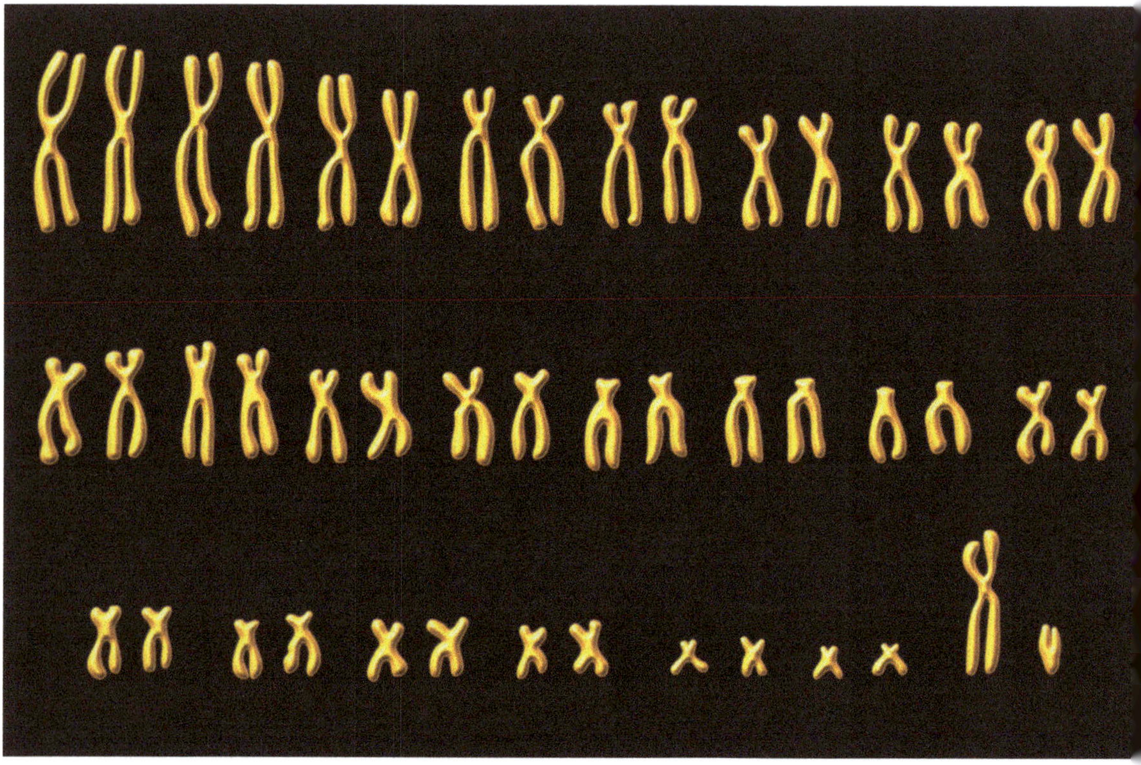

The twenty-two autosomes are nearly identical in size and composition. The sex chromosomes (*bottom row, far right*) are different sizes in males.

pairs are basically identical in males and females. These twenty-two chromosome pairs are called autosomes. The remaining pair, the sex chromosomes, is different in males and females. Females have two X chromosomes while males have one X chromosome and one Y chromosome.

Egg and sperm cells are different. These cells are called gametes. Gametes carry half of the DNA complement in twenty-three single chromosomes, which have been randomly selected. When fused, the egg and sperm create an embryo, or a fertilized cell. The embryo receives twenty-three chromosomes from each of its parents. Therefore, an offspring shares approximately 50 percent of its genetic sequence with its mother and 50 percent with its father. Each of the offspring's parents carry about half of each of their parents' DNA. Consequently, the offspring will share about 25 percent of its DNA sequence with each of its biological grandparents, approximately 12.5 percent with its great-grandparents, about 6.25 percent with its great-great grandparents, and so on.

Genealogical Versus Genetic Family Tree

Because the percentage of DNA passed through a family decreases with each generation, there are differences between genealogical and genetic family trees. A genealogical family tree contains every parent, grandparent, great-grandparent, great-great-grandparent, and so on back through history. In most cases, this family tree is the one that people think of when they think of genealogy. This type of family tree is constructed using paper records, such as birth and death certificates, census records, and newspapers to fill in a complete picture.

The second type of family tree is the genetic family tree. This family tree contains only those ancestors who contributed DNA

THE HUMAN GENOME PROJECT

The Human Genome Project (HGP) was an immense public and private competition to determine the exact sequence of all 3.2 billion base pairs found in the human genome. Between the project's inception in 1990 and its completion in 2003, computer hardware and software grew exponentially, increasing scientists' capacity to store and access bits of information. Out of necessity, the project also accelerated the development of methodologies needed to support the DNA sequencing process. This combined expansion of genetic knowledge, sequencing ability, and computer capacity allowed more segments of DNA to be sequenced with increasing speed and lower costs. Genetic genealogists today benefit from these technologies in the form of inexpensive DNA analysis, which allows them to compare the genomes of potential relatives.

to the individual trying to determine his or her ancestry. While the two trees overlap, not every person in the genealogical family tree will contribute segments of his or her DNA sequence to the test taker's DNA. Because parents only pass about 50 percent of their DNA to their children, segments of DNA are lost with each subsequent generation. Therefore, the genetic family tree contains far fewer ancestors than the genealogical one. However, the genetic family tree is a subset of the genealogical family tree.

The reason this situation occurs is because only one chromosome of a pair is selected to go into a sperm or an egg. The process of determining which chromosome is chosen for a specific sperm or egg is completely random. Which sperm fertilizes the egg is also up to chance. Imagine, for example, three siblings—Jackson, Jordan, and Jillian. The siblings' father, Michael, carries two different forms of a particular gene on each of his number three chromosomes. Assume these alleles are called 3a and 3b. Michael received allele 3a from his mother. He got 3b from his father. By chance, Jackson and Jillian both receive allele 3a from their father. Jordan gets allele 3b. If, in the future, a genetic genealogist were to look at only this particular chromosome, they would be able to trace all three siblings back to Michael. However, only Jordan could be traced back to Michael's father. If only the number three chromosomes were examined, Michael's mother would not appear in Jordan's genetic family tree at all, even though she is his biological grandmother. Of course genetic genealogists do not compare the sequences of only one section of DNA to determine family relationships, but this example illustrates how genealogical and genetic family trees can overlap, but they are not identical.

Immediate family members nearly always have some genetic segments in common. However, the more extended

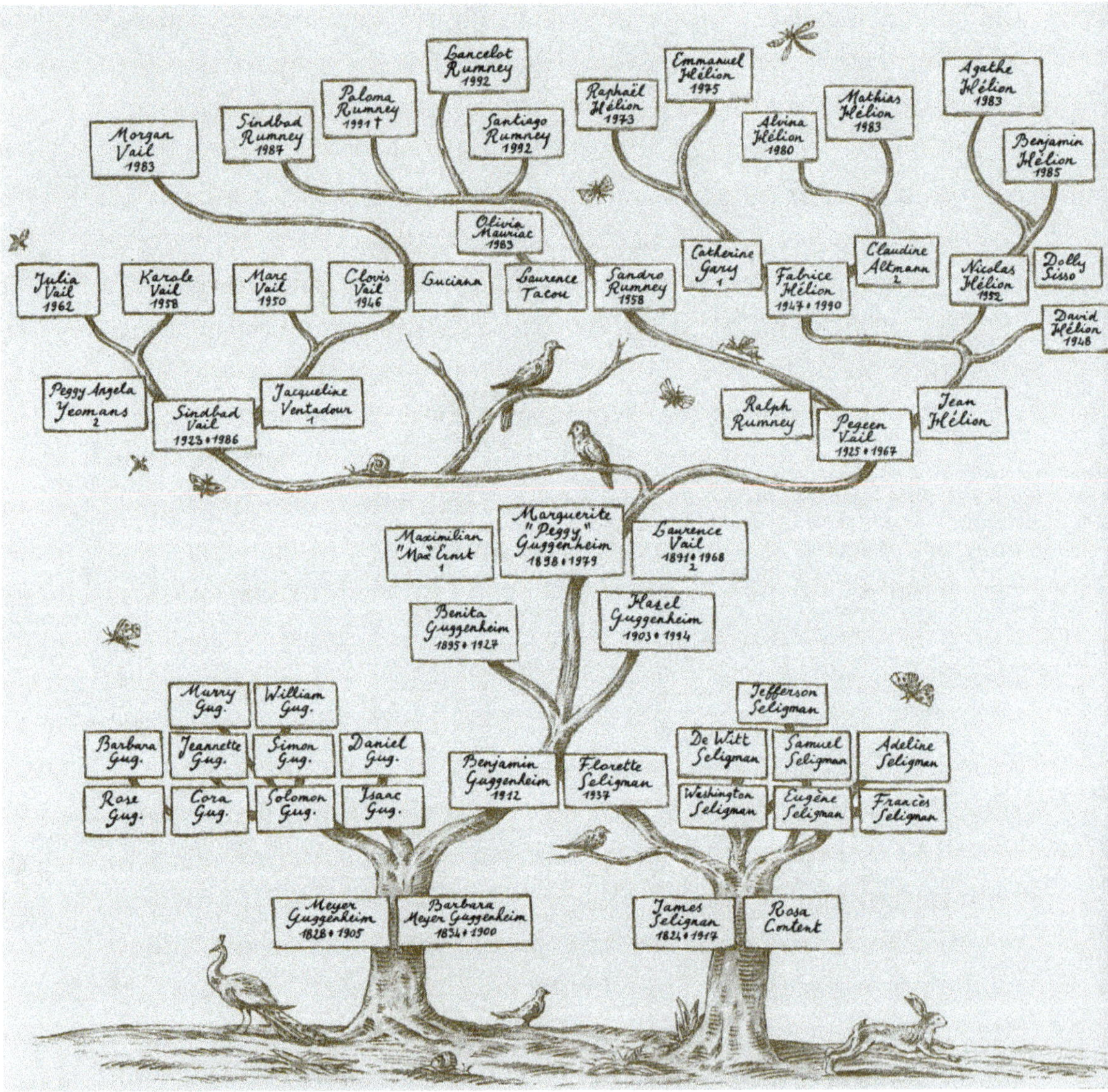

A genealogical family tree shows how individuals are related to one another through time. This family tree traces the descendants of American industrialist and philanthropist Meyer Guggenheim (1828–1905).

the relationship, the less likely this commonality becomes. It is entirely possible for two people on the same genealogical family tree to have genetic family trees that do not overlap at all. This lack of overlap does not mean they are not biologically related. It only means both of them did not inherit the same segments of DNA from their common ancestors.

Many people who get their DNA tested believe they will receive a list of all of their genealogical relatives from the testing company. Not understanding how DNA is passed from parent to offspring and that not all segments of DNA are tested, these people can end up being disappointed or disconcerted by their DNA results.

2 Genetic Ancestry Basics

When most people think of DNA testing, they think of television crime shows like *CSI* or *NCIS*. While DNA fingerprinting has certainly upended the criminal justice system, it can be useful in other circumstances, too. It can help doctors diagnose and guide treatment of some diseases while determining the likelihood of developing others. It can also establish paternity and other genetic relationships.

History of Genetic Genealogy

The history of human genetic understanding begins with Gregor Mendel's pea experiments in 1865. These experiments demonstrated that heredity was transmitted in discrete units, which Mendel (1822–1884) called particles. Today, these units are called genes. Even though Mendel was able to describe how some characteristics passed from one generation to the next, he did not understand how this inheritance occurred at the molecular level. It did not help that Mendel was a monk, not a scientist. His obscurity, as far as the scientific world was concerned, meant that his work was mostly ignored at the time of its publication. Nearly forty years passed before scientists realized its importance.

The nineteenth-century monk Gregor Mendel is often called the "father of modern genetics."

By the time Mendel's work was rediscovered, scientists had a much better understanding of the interworking of cells and how they divided. Two scientists, Walter Sutton (1877–1916) and Theodor Boveri (1862–1915), working independently, both discovered that Mendel's observations in pea plants and his descriptions of the inheritance of his so-called "particles" correlated precisely with the behavior of chromosomes during cell division. This realization led to the conclusion that genes were the units of heredity and that they were located on chromosomes. The chromosome theory of inheritance was proposed in 1902.

Although the DNA molecule was first isolated in 1869, scientists did not link it to heredity until 1944. Up to this point, it was thought that proteins, not DNA, carried genetic information. In 1953, Francis Crick (1916–2004) and James Watson (1928–) described the structure of DNA for the first time and, two years later, Arthur Kornberg (1918–2007) isolated an enzyme called DNA polymerase. DNA polymerase is essential for the sequencing of DNA. DNA sequencing, or the determination of the order of base pairs in a DNA molecule, occurred for the first time in 1975.

The National Institute of Health (NIH) established the first genetic database, containing the DNA sequences of a wide variety of organisms, in 1982. The NIH's database, called GenBank, is accessible to the public, and researchers still analyze data from its archives today.

In 1983, American biochemist Kary Mullis (1944–) developed a technique, called polymerase chain reaction (PCR), that allowed scientists to create billions of copies of specific DNA sequences in a matter of hours. This development greatly sped up the process of sequencing genomes and allowed the first human genetic map to be created in 1987.

DNA

DeoxyriboNucleic Acid

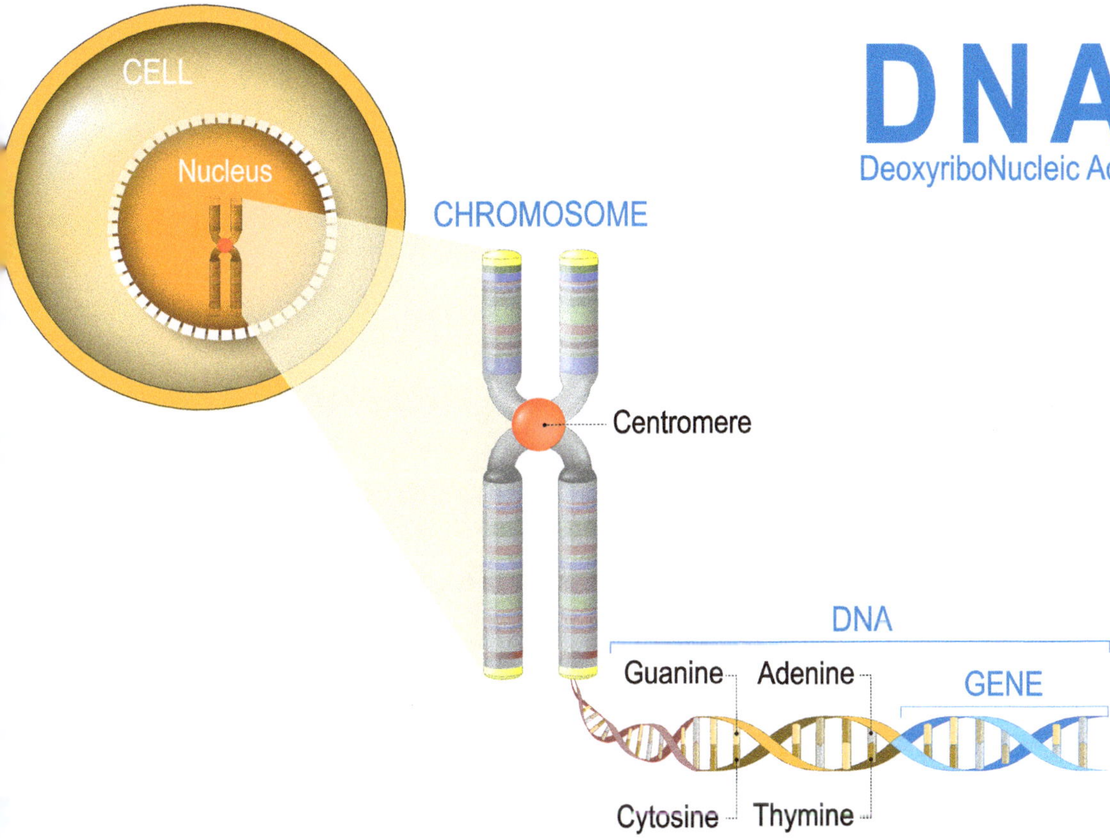

A gene is a section of DNA that codes for a particular trait. Genes are found on chromosomes.

GENEALOGY IN POPULAR CULTURE

Family traditions, reunions, and relationships are common themes in popular culture. Films, television shows, novels, advertisements, and documentaries capitalize on the yearning people feel for a family connection. Complex bloodlines along the path to Jedi mastery is, in part, what keeps fans returning to the ***Star Wars*** universe. Family history of muggle-born wizards, wizarding families, and squibs are part of the fascination people have with the world of Harry Potter. These concepts are also the basis for television shows such as ***Finding Your Roots***, ***Who Do You Think You Are?***, and ***Genealogy Roadshow***, all of which appeal to the interest in finding one's own roots, as well as watching the reactions of others as they find out where, and who, they came from.

DNA fingerprinting, or DNA profiling, as it is known today, was developed in the 1980s. DNA was first used in a criminal investigation in 1986. At that time, scientists required large amounts of high-quality DNA to produce accurate and reproducible results. Large quantities of DNA were not always available for recovery during forensics investigations, however. The development of PCR during the late 1980s greatly increased the sensitivity of DNA profiling methods and allowed DNA testing to be carried out on much smaller amounts of DNA.

In 1990, an effort called the Human Genome Project (HGP) was launched to sequence the estimated 3.2 billion base pairs contained within human DNA. Initially, the project was slated to be a fifteen-year-long effort. However, it was completed in 2003, two years ahead of schedule.

In 2000 Family Tree DNA became the first direct-to-consumer genetic testing company to offer DNA sequencing specifically for genealogy research. The first commercial testing was done on the Y chromosome, which is only found in males, and mitochondrial DNA, which is passed from mother to child.

The National Geographic Society, in partnership with IBM, began collecting and analyzing DNA of people from around the world in 2005. The purpose of their study, called the Genographic Project, was to map human migration patterns across the globe.

In 2007 the testing company 23andMe was the first to offer personal autosomal DNA testing. Family Tree DNA launched their own autosomal DNA tests in 2010, and AncestryDNA began offering the same test in 2012. Each company has their own proprietary database of DNA sequences. As of May 2017, the International Society of Genetic Genealogy (ISOGG) estimated that AncestryDNA had the largest number of people in their database, which consists of approximately five million test results.

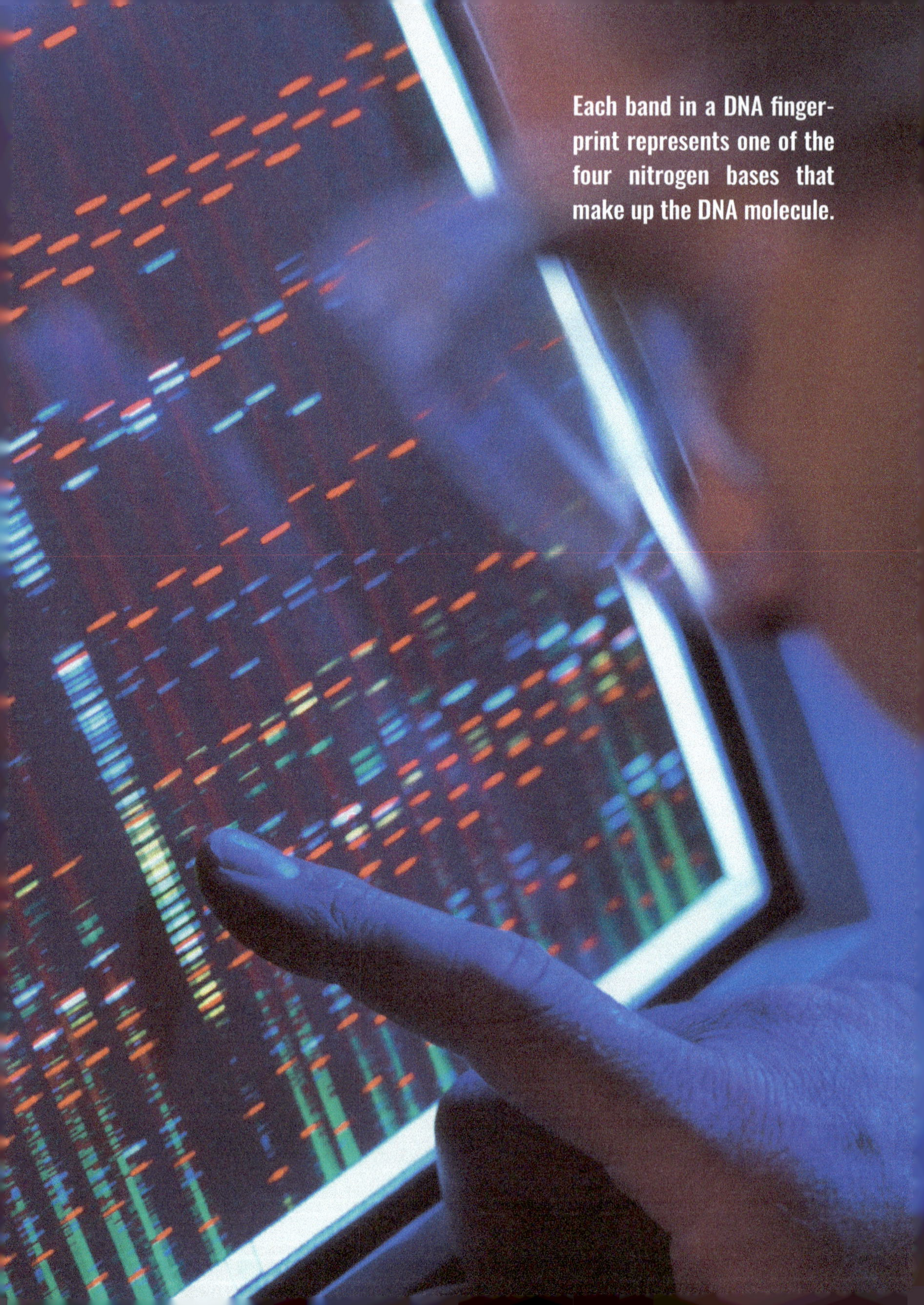

Each band in a DNA fingerprint represents one of the four nitrogen bases that make up the DNA molecule.

Understanding the Language of Genetic Testing

Most cells within the human body carry a complete set of nuclear and mitochondrial DNA. Therefore, nearly any cell can be retrieved and its DNA sequenced. Commercial testing companies collect skin cells from the inside of the cheek for testing. Obtaining skin cells is fairly straightforward. The selected company sends a testing kit that contains either cotton swabs or sterile collection tubes and a return envelope. If the testing kit includes cotton swabs, the test taker scrapes the inside of his or her cheek with a swab to collect cheek cells. This procedure is completely painless. The cotton swab is then placed inside a tube, which may contain an antibiotic fluid to prevent the growth of bacteria, and enclosed in the supplied return envelope.

Other companies have test takers collect a specified amount of saliva. Saliva contains skin cells that have been shed from the inside of the cheeks. Test takers spit repeatedly into the tube until the proper amount of saliva has been collected and return the tubes to the company. Test kits usually contain more than one swab or collection tube to ensure an adequate amount of DNA has been collected for the test. Testing fees range between $79 and $200, depending on the complexity of the test. Some companies include shipping in their prices, while others do not.

The most basic test is a twelve-marker test. A marker is simply a specific DNA sequence that has a known location in the genome. A twelve-marker test searches twelve specific areas of DNA. A thirty-seven-marker test is more advanced and, as its name implies, analyzes more areas. Generally speaking, the more markers a test searches for, the more expensive it is. At the same time, test takers are also more likely to find potential relatives using tests that probe more sections of DNA. Choosing which test

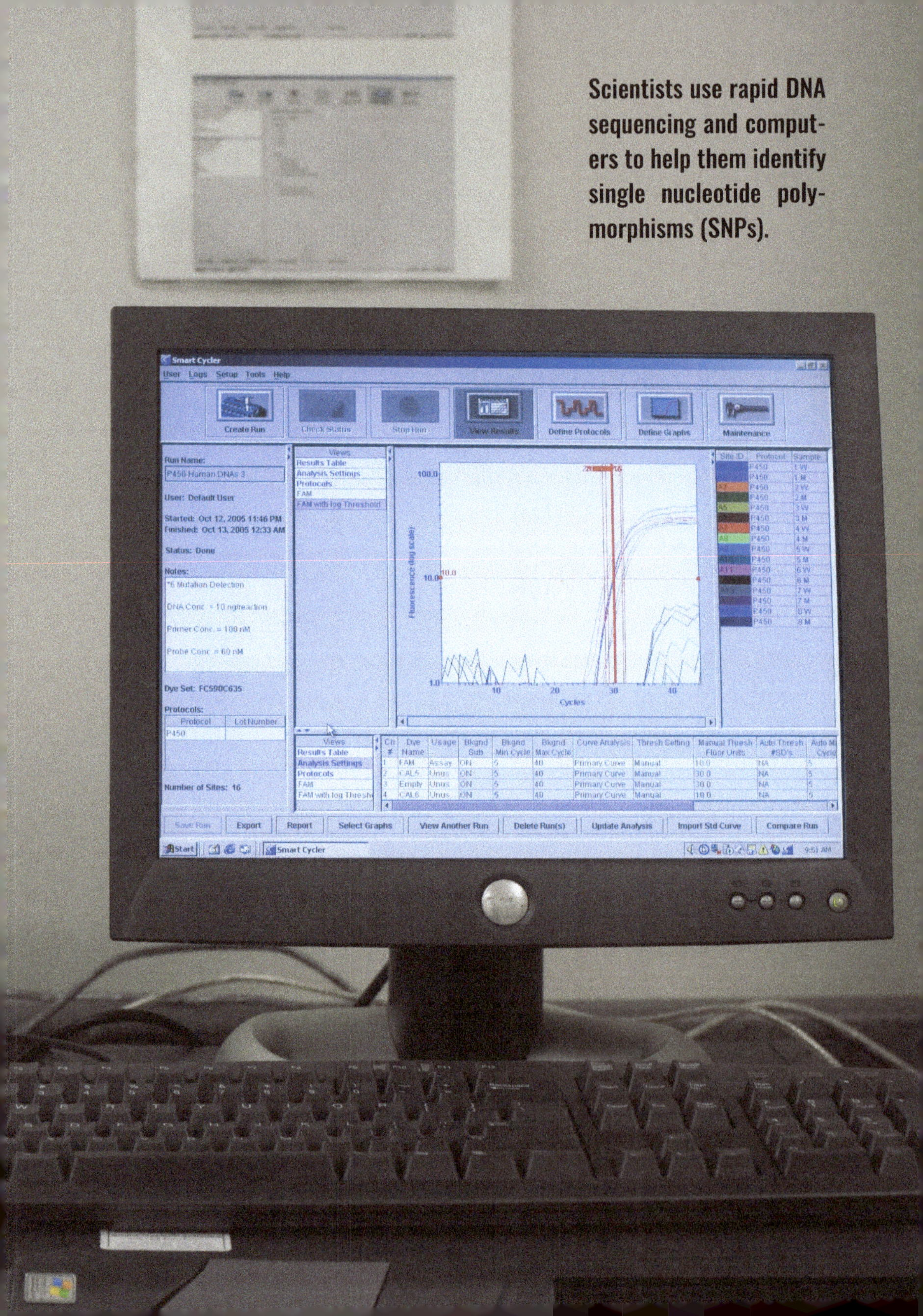

Scientists use rapid DNA sequencing and computers to help them identify single nucleotide polymorphisms (SNPs).

is best depends on the test taker's objectives. If he or she is only interested in determining where on the globe his or her family originated, a lower number of markers is probably sufficient. If, however, the test taker is determined to find out how distantly a specific person is related, a higher number of markers will likely be necessary.

Two terms that often come up in genetic testing are short tandem repeats (STRs) and single nucleotide polymorphisms (SNPs). Short tandem repeats are short sequences of two to five base pairs that repeat end to end to end, sometime thousands of times. For example, the tandem repeat "GAAAGAAAGAAAGAAA" represents four end-to-end repeats of the four-base pair sequence GAAA.

Although STRs can occur anywhere in nuclear DNA, genetic genealogists are mostly concerned with the STRs contained within the Y chromosome. STRs have been specifically useful in determining relationships within more recent time frames of up to five hundred years or so.

Single nucleotide polymorphisms, on the other hand, are differences found in a single DNA building block between two groups of people. There are roughly ten million SNPs in the human genome. SNPs usually occur between genes. These stretches of non-coding DNA were originally thought to be "junk" DNA, but scientists have since determined that they play a key role in the regulation of genes. Most SNPs have no effect whatsoever on the health or development of an individual. However, they can sometimes be helpful in predicting a person's response to certain kinds of drugs, his or her susceptibility to environmental factors, such as toxins, or the risk of developing a specific disease. As SNP tests become more comprehensive, they are becoming increasingly important in genetic genealogy.

SNPs occur much more rarely than STRs. Because SNPs tend to only occur once over long periods of time, they are very useful for determining at what point in the past two populations diverged into two different groups. Both STRs and SNPs are used to sort test takers into haplogroups. A haplogroup is a group of people who, at any point in the past, shared a common ancestor.

3

Types of Genetic Ancestry Tests

Most commercial genetic genealogy testing companies offer three types of DNA testing—Y-chromosomal DNA (Y-DNA) testing, mitochondrial DNA (mtDNA) testing, and autosomal DNA (atDNA) testing. Each type of test can reveal different relationships.

Y-chromosomal DNA (Y-DNA) Testing

The Y chromosome is one of the two sex chromosomes. Together with the X chromosome, it determines whether a person is biologically male or female. Females do not have a Y chromosome. They have two X chromosomes. Males, on the other hand, carry one X chromosome and one Y chromosome. Only the father can pass down a Y chromosome to produce a boy child. DNA contained within the Y chromosome can be used to trace the father's, or the paternal, ancestral line.

Unlike other chromosomes, the Y chromosome does not have a homologue, or another similar chromosome in the genome. During cell division, homologous chromosomes pair up and exchange genetic material in a process called crossing over. Crossing over creates unique recombinant chromosomes, which are passed down to the next generation creating different traits. Because the Y chromosome does not have a homologous chromosome in which to exchange material, it changes very little as it is passed down from father to son. The tips of the Y chromosome and the X chromosome sometimes cross over and recombine, but these areas are not used for genealogical research or haplogroup determination. As a result, the Y chromosome is uniquely suited for exploring ancient paternal lines.

Laboratories that perform Y-DNA testing for genealogical purposes test both slow-mutating markers and fast-mutating

Homologous chromosomes exchange genetic material during the creation of gametes.

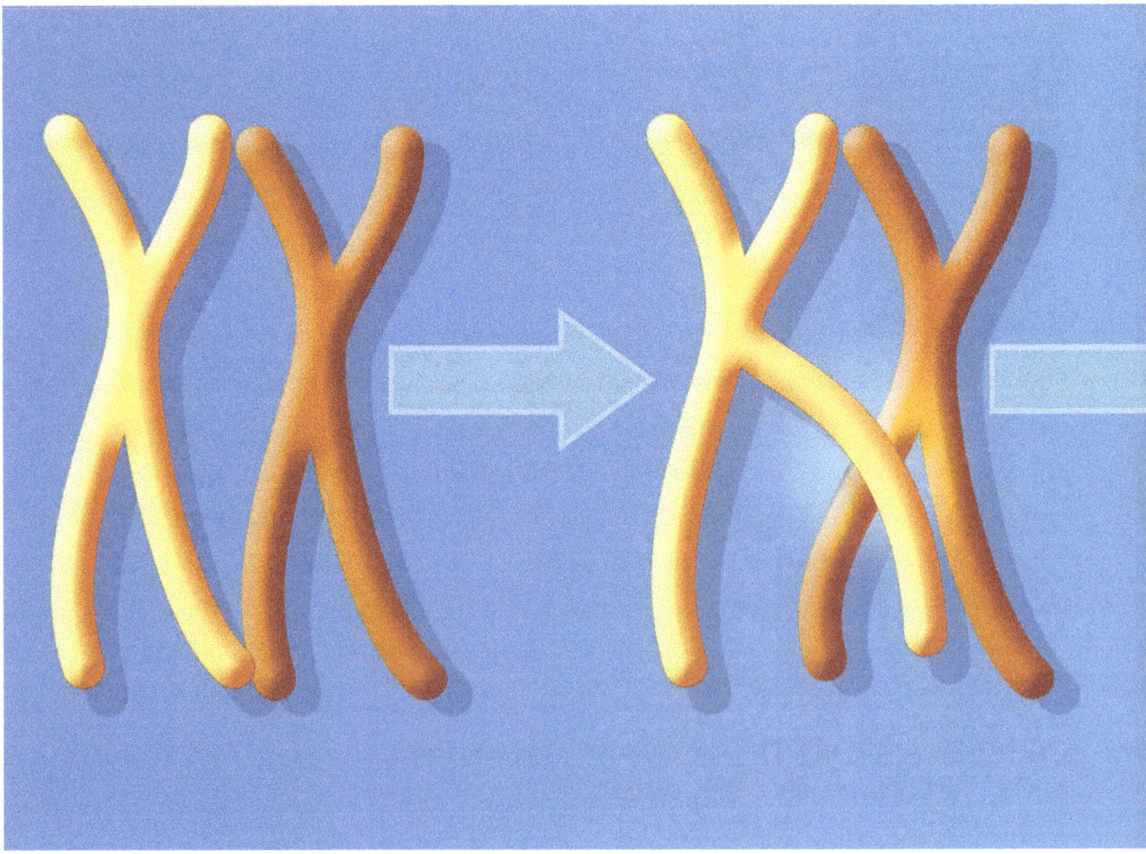

ones. Fast-mutating markers are ones that have changed in the last four hundred years or so. These markers are valuable for finding close relatives and differentiating between paternal lines. Slow-mutating markers, on the other hand, are important for determining deep ancestry. Deep ancestry reveals relationships many hundreds or thousands of years ago.

Most testing companies report the number of STRs at given locations along the Y chromosome. More and more SNPs are also being discovered and reported. The STR value for an individual is the number of times each sequence is repeated at the given location. The acronym DYS stands for DNA Y-chromosome

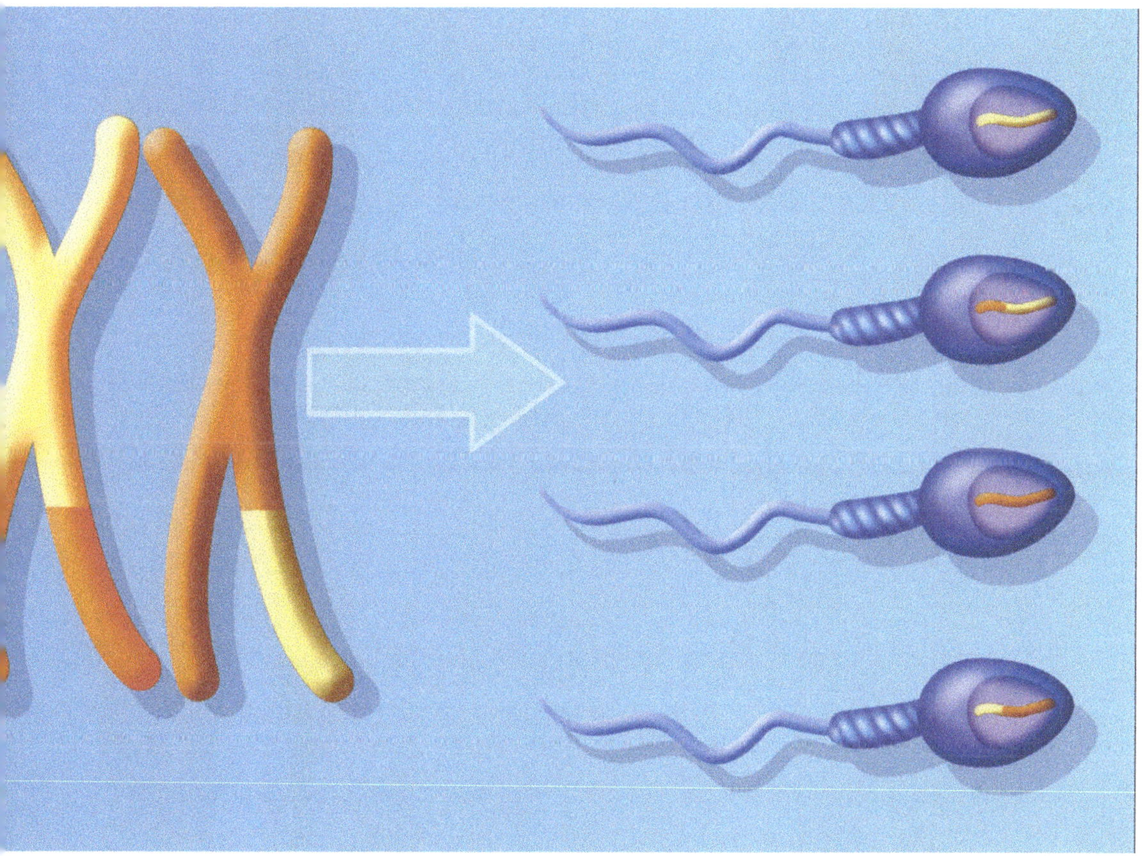

segment number. The DYS identifies the specific location, or locus, on the Y chromosome. For example, DYS 393 is a specific short tandem repeat located at position 393. For each DYS, a testing company will report a value. If, for example, the value at DYS 393 is fourteen, the test taker's Y chromosome has fourteen repeats of specific base pairs at locus 393.

These values are meaningless individually. They only take on significance when they are compared to the number of repeats other men have at the same locations. The more values two men share, the more closely related they are likely to be. Taken together, the number of repeats at each DYS represents a male's haplotype. Men closely related within recent centuries will most likely be members of the same haplogroup. Men that are not members of the same haplogroup are unlikely to be closely related.

SNPs are permanent single nucleotide changes in the genetic code. These mutations can be used to find junctions in the branches of a family tree and to trace human ancestors back through prehistory. Two men who share the same DNA sequence at a known Y-SNP site may share a close relative. Men who differ at two Y-SNP sites are likely to share a more recent common male ancestor than those who differ at ten Y-SNP sites. As the number of known Y-SNPs increase, their usefulness to genealogists will also increase.

Finding STR and SNP matches in a testing company's database depends on whether or not that person's paternal region of origin has been sampled. It is also possible for a paternal line to be wiped out by factors such as war, disease, or genetic disorders. Paternal lines may also end when men have only daughters, in which case, the man's Y chromosome is never passed to the next generation. This situation is called "daughtering out." The larger the database against which results are compared, the more likely a person will learn something useful about their family's history.

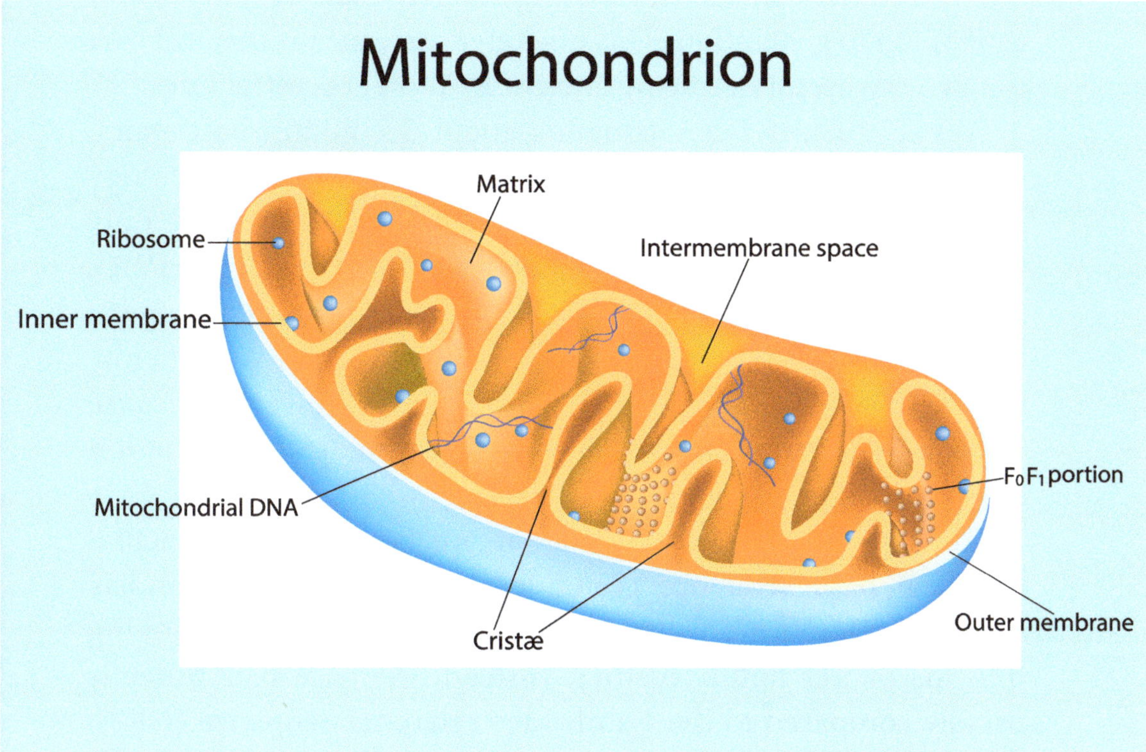

This diagram shows the different parts of a mitochondrion, including the mtDNA. Mitochondrial DNA is inherited only through the maternal line.

Mitochondrial DNA (mtDNA) Testing

Although most DNA is contained within the chromosomes of a cell's nucleus, a small amount can also be found in the mitochondria. Cells have differing numbers of mitochondria, depending on their function in the body. Red blood cells, for example, contain no mitochondria, whereas muscle and liver cells may have hundreds or even thousands of these tiny organelles.

Offspring, both daughters and sons, inherit their mitochondria exclusively through their mother's egg. Thus, it can be used to trace the mother's, or the maternal, lineage. Like Y-DNA, mtDNA is relatively stable, meaning that it changes very little from generation to generation. This unaltered state means that mtDNA can be very useful in tracing ancient maternal ancestral lines.

While nuclear DNA contains about 3.2 billion base pairs, mtDNA consists of only about 16,500 or so. A genetic genealogy company may sequence the entire mtDNA molecule or only two non-coding regions called hyper variable regions (HVR). Sequencing only HVR1 and HVR2 is often of limited genealogical use. Therefore, many companies offer full mtDNA sequencing. This decision is not something to take lightly, however, because the coding regions of mtDNA may reveal medical information as well as genealogical data.

Testing companies do not normally report the actual chemical base sequence contained within the mitochondria since this would be of limited usefulness to someone looking into his or her family history. Instead, the base pair order is usually compared to the Cambridge reference sequence (CRS). The CRS is the mtDNA sequence of a European woman, which was first published in the 1980s. Test takers of European descent usually have mtDNA sequences that differ very little from the CRS. Thus, test results often list only the differences. For example, a test result may contain the notation 111T, 319A, and 362C in HVR1. This result means that the test taker's mtDNA differs from the reference sequence at base pair numbers 16,111; 16,319; and 16,362. The 16,000 is dropped for convenience in reporting. The letters T, A, and C refer to thymine, adenine, and cytosine, respectively.

Mitochondrial DNA testing has been very useful in helping historians sort out mysteries from the past. In 2014 archaeologists from the University of Leicester successfully sequenced the mtDNA of a skeleton found in 2012. The bones

Y-CHROMOSOMAL ADAM AND MITOCHONDRIAL EVE

If all the men on Earth were to trace their paternal lines back in time, they would all merge on a single man that scientists call Y-chromosomal Adam. The identity of Y-chromosomal Adam is not known but, based on the number of mutations found in modern-day Y chromosomes and knowledge of the mutation rate in Y-DNA, scientists estimate that he probably lived about two hundred thousand to three hundred thousand years ago.

Likewise, all humans can trace their maternal lines back to a single woman called Mitochondrial Eve. Mitochondrial Eve is the mtDNA ancestor of all living humans. Based on the mutations found in modern-day mtDNA and known mutation rates, scientists believe Mitochondrial Eve likely lived about one hundred thousand to two hundred thousand years ago.

Although their names come from the Bible, neither Y-chromosomal Adam nor Mitochondrial Eve were the only man and woman alive at the time. Neither were they the only ones to have offspring. However, at some time between then and now, those other men's and women's lines died out.

were the suspected remains of King Richard III (1452–1485) of England. After comparing the mtDNA sequence found in the bones with the mtDNA sequence of a known descendant of King Richard III's sister Anne, the identification was confirmed.

Y-DNA was used in a similar case to establish a link between President Thomas Jefferson (1743–1826) and the son of one of Jefferson's slaves, Sally Hemings (1773–1835). Oral traditions in the Hemings family suggested that Jefferson fathered one of the young slave's children. For many years, historians and heirs of Jefferson denied any affair between Jefferson and Hemings. Instead, the Jefferson heirs explained that one of Jefferson's nephews fathered one of Hemings's children.

In 1998 Dr. Eugene Foster traced four male lineages—two of Jefferson's nephews and two of Sally Hemings's sons. Hemings had other children, but only her oldest son, Thomas Woodson, and her youngest, Eston Hemings Jefferson, had living male heirs. Foster, with the help of population geneticist Christopher Tyler-Smith, analyzed the DNA found in the Y chromosome of the Jeffersonian lineage. They found a distinct set of mutations that are very rare in the general population. Since Y chromosomes are passed down from father to son, if Jefferson was indeed the father of Hemings's son, it was likely that the son would carry the same mutations. The nephews tested came from Jefferson's sister's side of the family. Jefferson's sister Martha was married to a man named Dabney Carr. Three descendants of Carr were tested. Their Y chromosomes were nearly identical to each other, but they were very different from the Jeffersonian Y chromosome. The Y-DNA sequence of Sally Hemings's youngest son, Eston, however, was nearly identical to that of Jefferson's. This test ruled out the possibility of one of the

Y-DNA testing can be used to establish paternity. It proved that Thomas Jefferson fathered at least one son with Sally Hemings, one of his slaves.

nephews fathering Eston and proved, with 99 percent accuracy, that Jefferson was Eston's father.

Autosomal DNA (atDNA) Testing

While mtDNA can trace a person's ancestry from his or her mother to her mother to her mother (and so on) and Y-DNA can trace the paternal line from a person's father to his father to his father (and so on), there are some obvious limitations. Chief among these limitations is the fact that the rest of the person's ancestors, his or her father's mother or mother's father, for example, will be excluded from the lineage analysis. To capture information about ancestors that are not in a strict maternal or paternal lineage, genetic genealogists rely on autosomal DNA (atDNA) testing. As its name implies, atDNA testing analyzes the twenty-two autosomes contained in a person's genome.

Autosomal DNA tests can identify close familial relationships, up to about the third or fourth cousin level, quite accurately. As relationships become more distant, however, the test's effectiveness decreases. The reason for this decline is that it is rare for distant relatives to inherit the exact same stretch of DNA from a shared ancestor. Remember that DNA sequences can be swapped between homologous chromosomes and chromosomes in a chromosome pair are randomly selected for inclusion in an egg or sperm. These factors mean that, over time, sequences linking close relatives often fail to transfer through the generations.

Autosomal DNA can change significantly, and often unpredictably, from one generation to the next. Companies that offer atDNA testing usually report the length of matching segments shared by two people. The longer the matching segment, the more closely the two are related.

For people who are interested in preserving information about their genetic family trees, it may be helpful to collect DNA carried by the family's oldest generation while it is still possible. Much of their DNA will likely have been inherited by descendants, but some of it will not and some of it may be different. These conditions can make reconstructing DNA connections at a later date much harder, if not impossible.

4

Genetic Ancestry Testing and Ethnicity

Most of the DNA sequence is the same in all humans. Scientists believe the reason for these similarities lies in the fact that all humans descended from a small *Homo sapiens* population that originated in Africa tens of thousands of years ago. However, over time, variations in DNA sequence, or mutations, arose and changed with different frequencies in different populations as our human ancestors migrated across the globe.

Ethnicity Estimates

All the major genetic genealogy testing companies provide test takers a report that informs them of their geographical origins based on the DNA variations they carry. However, each company calls this report something different, including Ancestry Composition (23andMe), Population Finder (Family Tree DNA), and Genetic Ethnicity (AncestryDNA). Scientists tend to call this estimation admixture or biogeographical ancestry analysis.

The term "ethnicity" means to belong to a social group that has specific cultural traditions. Some people confuse ethnicity

An early human shows his sons how to construct stone tools. All humans belong to the species *Homo sapiens. Homo sapiens* evolved in Africa about two hundred thousand years ago.

This woman is Hmong, an ethnic group from China and Southeast Asia. Most people would categorize her race as Asian. But race is a social classification system. It places people into groups based on observable physical features, such as skin color and facial structure. These categories are not recognizable on a genetic level.

with race. However, race is generally associated with physical features while ethnicity describes a cultural identity.

Regardless of what it is called, these estimations all determine the same thing—where the test taker's DNA fits into one or more world populations based on comparisons of DNA segments present in reference samples. When a test taker's DNA sequence matches a segment in the reference population, the test taker is assigned to that group on the assumption that the DNA likely came from that population at some time in the past. To create an admixture, all the populations the test taker's DNA matches are aggregated, or combined, to form an overall biogeographical ancestry estimate.

Depending on the testing company and, more precisely, the ethnic makeup of their reference populations, a test taker may find out generally where his or her ancestors originated. For example, test results may show that a test taker is mainly of European descent. He or she may also have a certain number of DNA matches within the African, Asian, and/or Native American populations as well.

Some companies get more specific and can provide likely countries, such as Scandinavia, Italy, Great Britain, and so on. The difference in specificity usually depends on the depth and breath of the testing company's reference populations, or the number of samples in their database and where the people providing those samples came from.

Ethnicity estimates face three challenges. First, the statistical methods used to determine them are still maturing. This emergence means that different companies use different methods to arrive at a possible conclusion about a person's overall biogeographical ancestry even when the analysis is applied to the same DNA sequence. The underlying data and calculations may be fact, but their interpretations are subjective because different assumptions are made.

The second challenge scientists face when trying to determine biogeographical ancestry is that the human genome only includes the DNA from a small portion of our distant ancestors. Think of it this way, ten generations ago, which covers approximately two hundred fifty years, every person had more than one thousand ancestors. Twenty generations, or about five hundred years ago, each person had more than a million ancestors, and only a subset of those ancestors actually passed along DNA that can be found in an individual test taker.

The third problem facing ethnicity estimates, at this time, is the size of the population databases to which a test taker's DNA is compared. Some databases oversample specific ethnicities while under-sampling or leaving out other ones altogether. For example, genetic genealogy companies have sampled the DNA of more people in Europe and North America than they have people who originated from other regions. This overrepresentation means that they have more information about possible DNA variations in these populations. If a test taker happens to have ancestors who originated from these areas, the test taker's admixture is likely to be quite reliable. However, if the test taker's ancestors came from South America, Africa, Asia, Australia, or Oceania, the estimate will not be as accurate. As more people get their DNA tested, reference populations will grow larger and, hopefully, more diverse. Until then, admixture results should be used to look for trends or patterns, not exact predictions.

Human Migration

Over the course of thousands of years, minor changes in the DNA passed from parent to child accumulate. By tracing these mutations back through time, genetic genealogists and anthropologists can determine at what point in a family tree a new branch was formed. People with the same mutations belong to the same haplogroup. Eventually, a mutation will occur within a haplogroup and be passed down to the next generation. When this occurs, a new haplogroup is formed.

By following the breadcrumb trail of branching haplogroups, scientists have been able to determine the migration patterns of ancient humans. So far, the data shows that as of seventy thousand years ago, all humans lived in Africa. Then, about sixty thousand years ago, scientists believe they began to migrate outward and, eventually, spread to the rest of the globe.

There is some evidence showing a major climatic shift occurred around seventy thousand years ago. Scientists believe this change in weather patterns may have driven the migration out of Africa. Genetic evidence left behind in modern-day humans points to a sharp decline in populations around this time. Scientists believe the number of *Homo sapiens* may have reached as low as ten thousand individuals. Once the climate stabilized, the population rebounded and began to expand outward, beyond Africa toward the Eurasian continent.

Arriving on the Arabian Peninsula, these intrepid explorers appear to have separated into two groups. One group spread along the Arabian Gulf coast and into India. Patterns of genetic mutations show that this group reached Southeast Asia and Australia about fifty thousand years ago. The second group ventured into the Middle East and southern Central Asia. This group eventually populated Europe and northern Asia. Then, around twenty thousand years ago, northern Mongolian hunters traveled across a land bridge that separated modern-day Siberia and Alaska to become the first people living in North America.

Limitations of Ethnicity Estimates

One thing that people who are looking into their genetic ancestry should keep in mind is that ethnicity estimates are exactly that—estimates. So far, DNA testing has only proved that Americans have very mixed backgrounds. To some, this comes as no surprise. However, to others, it upends their entire sense of self.

Mainly, test takers need to understand that current reference populations are of limited sample size and are not representative

Modern humans migrated out of Africa (*green*) about seventy thousand years ago and into Europe and Asia. They reached Australia via an island chain (*orange*). The turquoise area indicates Ice Age glaciers (fifty-five thousand to fifteen thousand years ago) that slowed down migration north and east until people crossed the land bridge (*blue*) into North America.

MAJOR HAPLOGROUPS

Y-DNA tests reveal paternal haplotypes while mtDNA tests place the test taker in a maternal one. The table shows some of the major haplogroups and what they reveal about an ancestor's origins.

Y-DNA Haplogroups	mtDNA	Significance
A, B, E	L, M, N	Root African haplogroups. Y-DNA haplogroup E3a most common lineage among African Americans.
R	R, H, I	R1b most common Y-DNA haplogroup in European populations. mtDNA haplogroup R gave rise to haplogroups H, I, and other European haplogroups.
Q	A, B, C, D	These haplogroups link northern and central Asian populations with Native Americans. Y-DNA Q3 haplogroup is strictly associated with Native American ancestry.

of people from all parts of the world. This means that almost certainly, any ethnicity estimate received today will be revised and updated in the future as more and more people get tested.

Another thing to take into account about admixtures is that some ethnicities cannot be accurately identified. For example, scientists have not found significant genetic differences between populations in modern-day Germany, France, Belgium, Switzerland, and a variety of other European countries that would allow them to reliably identify an individual as belonging to just one of those populations. However, with the understanding of these limitations, some of the information gathered about possible ethnic identities could be useful in directing a test taker to areas of their family history they had not considered.

5

Ethics of Genetic Genealogy

While traditional genealogical research can often reveal lost stories in a family's history, genetic genealogy is capable of revealing family secrets—secrets that may have been kept for a good reason. Before ordering a DNA test for genealogical purposes, potential test takers should think about possible outcomes that might cause others pain or distress and how these unintended consequences could be handled.

Understanding Potential Consequences

Most people who delve into their genetic genealogy do so on impulse. They believe the results will be fun and interesting and, for the most part, that is exactly what they find. However, some people find out more about their family history than they bargained. Suppose, for example, a genetic genealogy company reports that a test taker's DNA is a 50 percent match with someone else's in their database. How might these two people be related? If there is a 50 percent match, the person in the company's database is likely to be the test taker's parent or sibling. Now, maybe the test taker knows this person. But it is possible that they do not.

Ancestry DNA testing could uncover unexpected relationships. Some people may be happy to find a long lost relative. Others may not react so positively to having their lives changed this way.

Before swabbing a cheek, it would behoove every DNA test taker to think about how he or she would react if they were to find a sibling or half-sibling they have never heard of. How might this knowledge impact the relationship with the test taker's parents? And what about the long-lost sibling? Would the test taker approach this person?

What if the test taker were approached by someone who is in some way related to them? Suppose this person is a probable first cousin. This result would mean that an aunt or an uncle had a child that the rest of the family, for whatever reason, does not know about. Should the test taker share this information with the rest of the family? Should the test taker ask the genetic relative to drop his or her inquiries? Should they ignore the person?

What if that person is an adoptee looking for his or her medical information? Is the test taker obligated to help this genetic relative? What if the family has a specific disease that they know is passed from parent to child? Should that make a difference in how the test taker interacts with potential relatives?

Test takers may also discover siblings or first cousins with whom they do not share any genetic information. This situation could reveal that family members are not biologically related.

Another thing to consider is how these situations might complicate inheritance issues. If a legal adoption occurred, there may be no repercussions in finding unexpected relations. However, state laws differ and if the circumstances of the child's birth did not lead to adoption, it is possible for the newly discovered family member to challenge an inheritance claim.

Other considerations include reproductive assistance, adoption, and second families. Egg and sperm donors often donate gametes to help infertile couples conceive. These people may go on to have families of their own. In addition, women, and

Adoptees may want to find their birth families to obtain medical or other information. However, how their search might affect other people's lives should also be considered.

their partners, give up children for adoption for many reasons, often good ones, and then go on with their lives. Think about how these people, through no fault of their own, might have their lives upended by someone else deciding to take a DNA test and finding a genetic link. Is it fair to approach someone who did not choose to dig into his or her family history?

There is no right or wrong answer to these questions. However, test takers should realize that undertaking a DNA test is not solely an individual decision. Every person carries bits and pieces of other's DNA in their own. Test takers are not only revealing their own history, but also the histories of others in their genetic family. Sometimes it may be better to let secrets remain secrets.

Implications of Unexpected Ethnicity

In the late nineteenth and early twentieth centuries, much of the genealogical research that was conducted was used to prove the pedigree necessary to join hereditary societies such as the Daughters of the American Revolution (DAR), the General Society of Mayflower Descendants, or the Plantagenet Medieval Society. Often, people interested in joining such societies have been brought up to view themselves as part of these cultures. Finding out their ethnicity differs from their upbringing can be psychologically difficult. On the other hand, some people believe that a DNA test can prove them "pureblooded."

This idea that certain DNA sequences can make some people exceptional implies that anyone without those specific markers is inferior. Exceptionalism is a concept that has been used and claimed by many to justify being treated differently. Claims of any ethnic, religious, or political group can be considered somehow "chosen." This mentality divides people on many scales, including

GENETIC GENEALOGY CAREERS

Genealogy is a very popular topic, but for the most part, people tend to do their own research into their family's history. For this reason, growth in the field of professional genealogist is projected to be minimal. The largest demand for qualified genealogists comes from law offices seeking to identify kinship in a legal context. Other employment opportunities may include the establishment of bloodlines and family connections for organizations in which pedigrees are required for membership. Other professional genealogists are hired to compile the family histories of a community or for assisting in the research efforts of writers, filmmakers, and historians.

Very few colleges offer genealogy courses and even fewer award degrees in the subject. However, the Board for Certification of Genealogists (BCG) offers several levels of certification and licensing. Taking advantage of this training could lead to a career as a professional genealogist.

geographically and culturally. As a whole, DNA proves that all humans are essentially the same. At a molecular level, people's differences are minute.

Regardless, there is a question as to how genetic ethnicity tests should be used. Should a light-skinned person, brought up as Caucasian and afforded all of the privileges of being white,

Members of the Plantagenet Medieval Society perform a medieval dance at Warkworth Castle in Northumberland, England. To become part of this organization, one must prove that they are descendants of one or more of the Plantagenet kings of England.

be able to take advantage of programs intended to counteract the discrimination toward minorities if a DNA test reveals the presence of African ancestry? Should someone with Native American ancestry be afforded tribal enrollment, even if he or she is not active in Native American culture?

These may sound like trivial questions. Who cares if someone is listed on a Native American tribal roll or if a seemingly white person has a small percentage of African heritage? But these questions take on more significance when asking who is allowed access to scholarships, jobs, and possible reparations for past injustices.

DNA Testing and Forensics

The arrival of forensic DNA testing to prove the guilt or innocence of criminal suspects was no doubt a boon to law enforcement agencies. Used correctly, DNA evidence can identify, with a very small margin of error, the people who were present at the scene of a crime including, possibly, the person who committed it. DNA evidence has also be used to exonerate, or clear, innocent people.

But some people are concerned about police access to private genealogical databases. When does the need for public safety supersede individual rights? Should law enforcement be allowed to search DNA databases for possible matches to DNA left behind at a crime scene?

What if someone's grandchild decided to trace their roots through genetic testing? Could his or her grandmother or grandfather go to prison if their DNA matched DNA left behind at a crime scene? What if the crime in question was committed decades ago? Should that make a difference?

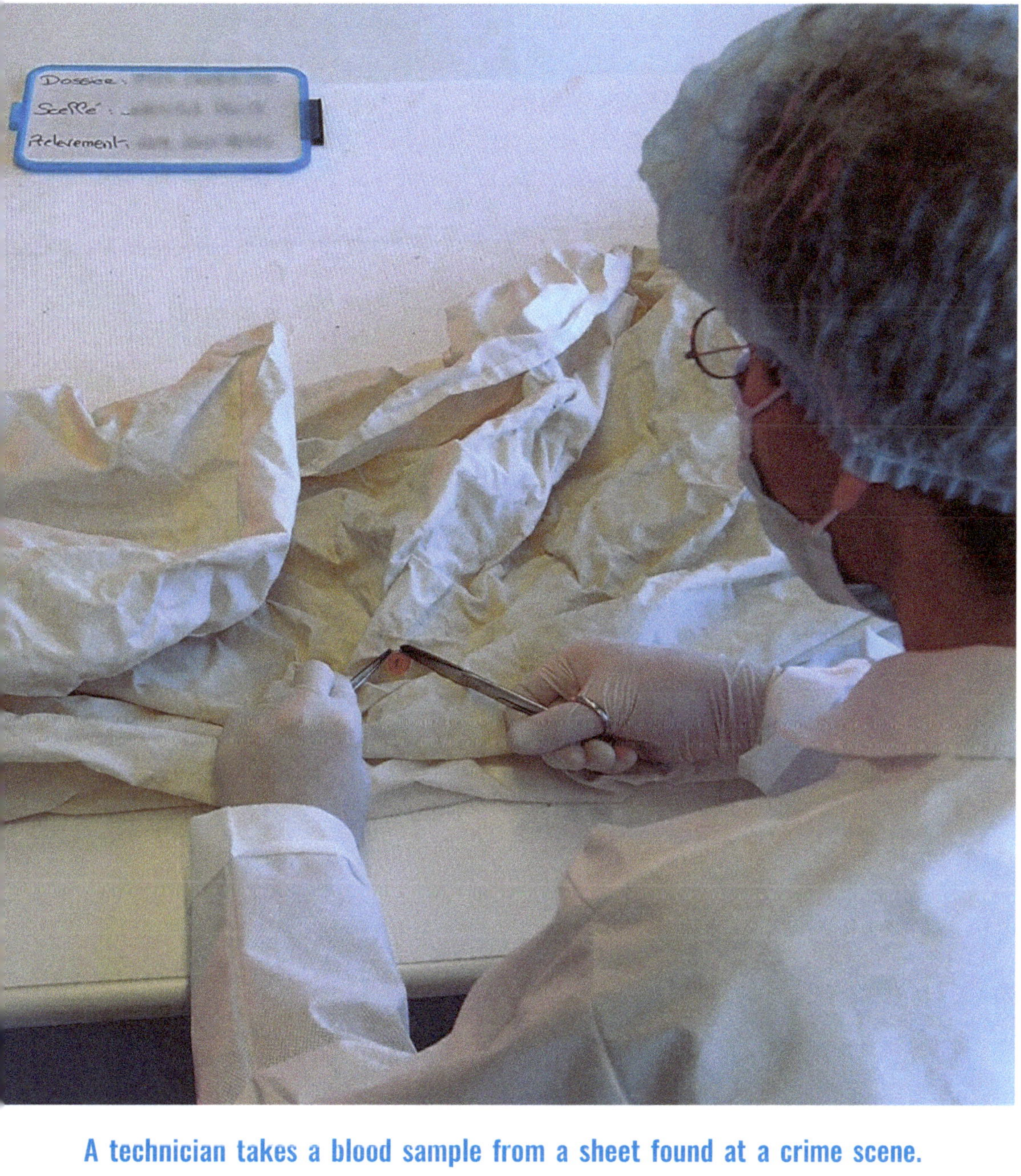

A technician takes a blood sample from a sheet found at a crime scene. Blood and other bodily fluids contain DNA. Evidence gathered from a crime scene can help police identify the person who committed the crime.

People sometimes answer these questions differently when they consider society as a whole versus their own family members. Other people do not believe it could happen in their families yet, it does. Test takers, and their relatives, should understand that every DNA result uploaded to a database could provide law enforcement with another opportunity to solve a cold case.

6

The Future of DNA Testing

DNA profiles not only contain private information about genetic relationships, but also about the test taker's health. Many people are concerned about how this data may be used in the future. As a society, people need to decide who can have access to private DNA data and how that data should be used.

DNA Testing and Health Information

Some genetic diseases can have disastrous effects on a person's future. Take Huntington's disease, for example. Huntington's is a fatal genetic disease in which the nerve cells in the brain deteriorate. This breakdown of nervous tissue effects movement, behavior, and thought processes. Symptoms of the disease usually begin to manifest between the ages of thirty-five and fifty-five. There is no cure.

Huntington's results from autosomal dominant inheritance. This inheritance pattern means that only one copy of the faulty gene is necessary for a person to develop the disease. Remember that each person gets two copies of every gene—one from his or her father and one from their mother. If one parent is affected with Huntington's disease, a child will either inherit the chromosome that carries the gene for Huntington's or they will inherit the normal one. Therefore, every child who has a parent with Huntington's disease has a fifty-fifty chance of inheriting the damaged gene and developing the disease themselves.

Researchers identified the gene that causes Huntington's disease in 1993. The fact that the disease has no cure means that people with an affected parent have a difficult choice to make: Should they have genetic testing done to determine if they carry the gene for Huntington's or not? If someone with a family history

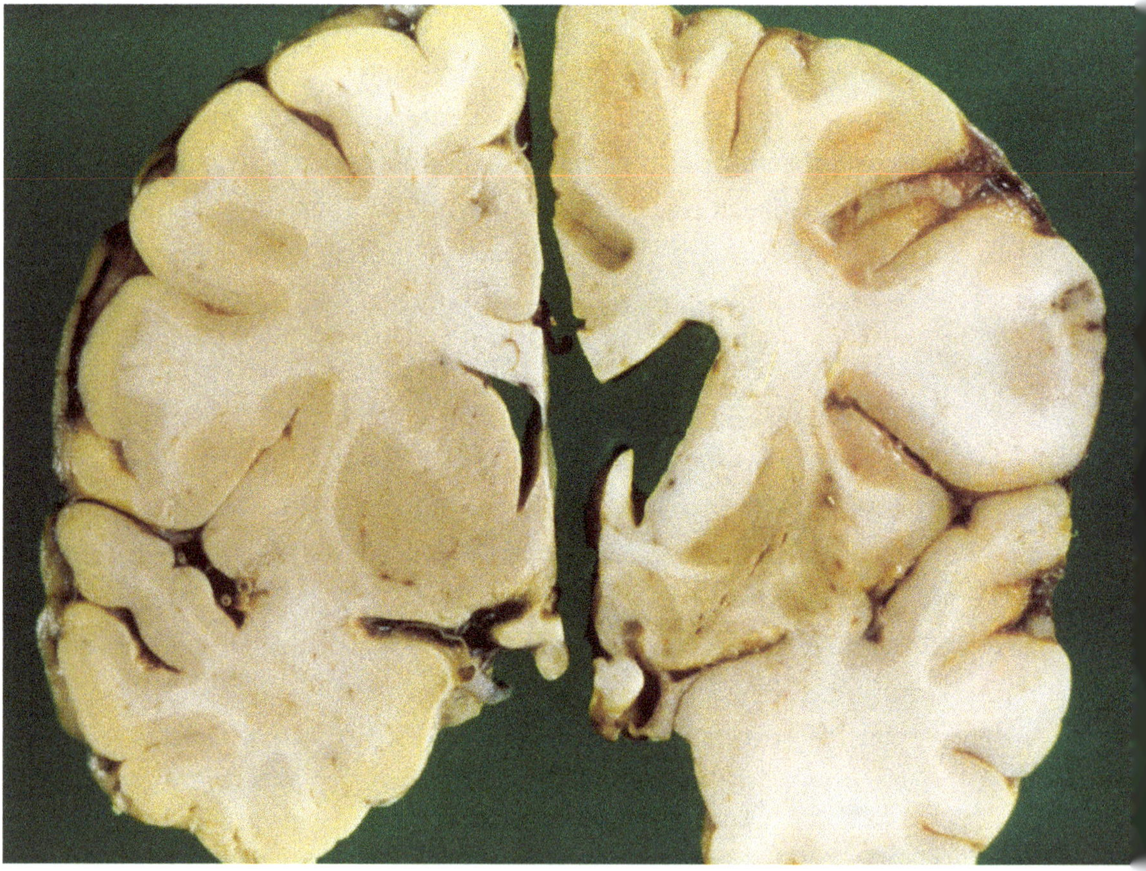

A comparison of normal brain tissue (*left*) and brain tissue from someone affected by Huntington's disease (*right*) displays the deterioration caused by the condition.

of Huntington's has DNA testing done for genealogical purposes and discovers relatives they did not know about, is that person obligated to alert these new relations to the family's history of genetic disease?

Huntington's is just one example of the potential health risks that can be revealed with DNA testing. Currently, 23andMe is the only genealogical testing company permitted by the Food and Drug Administration (FDA) to provide an assessment of genetic health risks. The company does not test for Huntington's, but it does look for genes associated with Alzheimer's disease, Parkinson's disease, age-related macular degeneration, and seven others. The presence of a gene variant does not necessarily mean that the test taker will develop one of the diseases the company tests for, but it may mean they have a higher risk than someone who does not carry an altered gene.

DNA Testing and Privacy

Some people are concerned with how genetic information could be used and who would have access to it. For example, DNA testing could be very beneficial to a person's medical team. It could alert a doctor to be on the look out for specific symptoms of a disease the person has an increased risk of developing. However, should that person's insurance company have access to this data? And, if they were granted access, should they be allowed to charge the person higher rates because he or she may develop a disease? Should they be allowed to deny that person coverage?

Should someone's employer have access to their DNA profile? Would a company invest in the future of an employee they know has the gene for Huntington's and will likely get sick in their late thirties or forties? The inability to get hired or to earn a promotion could greatly affect a person's ability to earn money before they

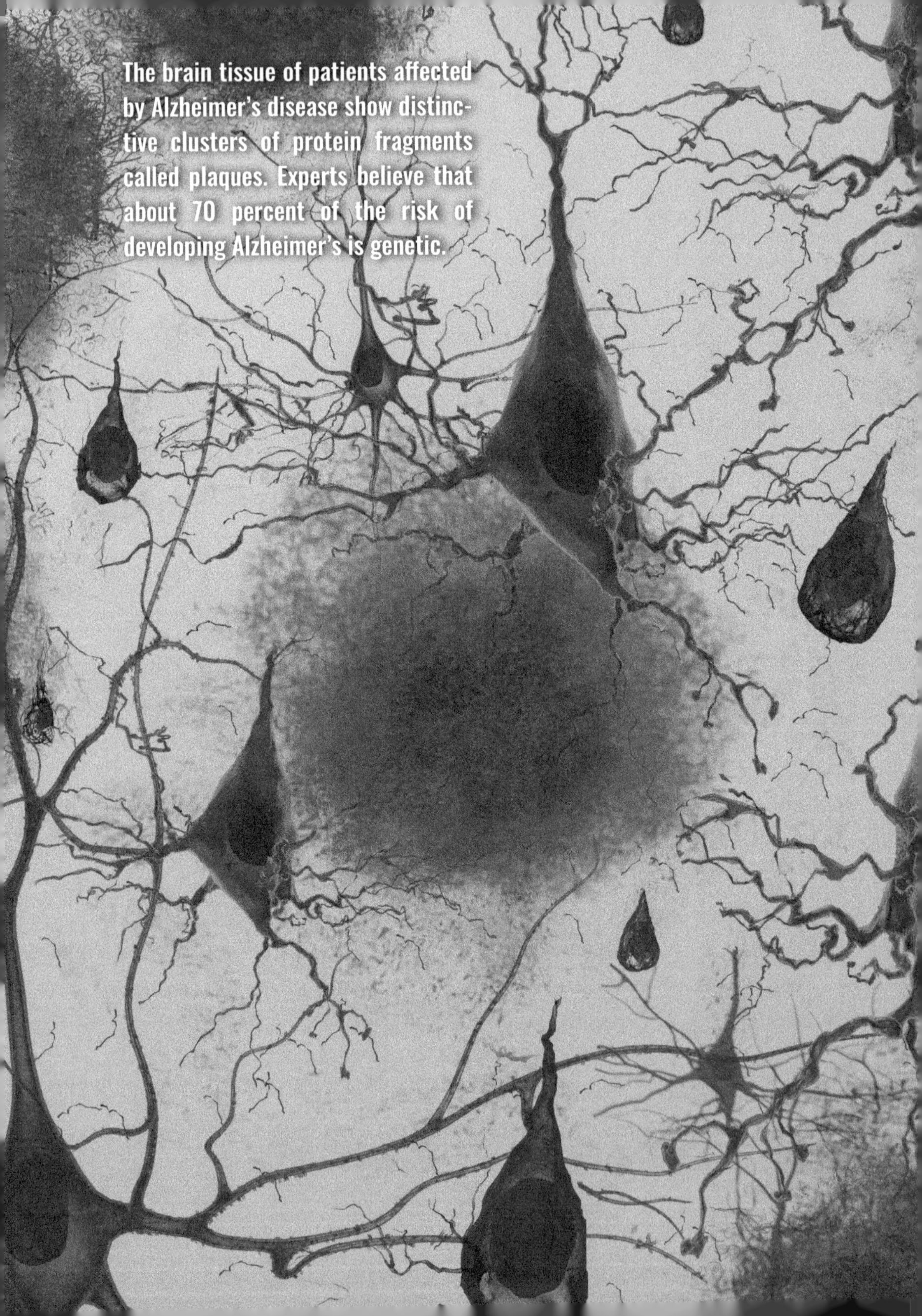

The brain tissue of patients affected by Alzheimer's disease show distinctive clusters of protein fragments called plaques. Experts believe that about 70 percent of the risk of developing Alzheimer's is genetic.

get sick. The decreased income could hamper their efforts to save enough for future medical procedures and to take care of their families after they are gone.

Many genetic ancestry companies will store test taker's DNA. Some charge more for this service, while it is included in the price of others. Test takers should contemplate whether or not they would like their DNA to be stored. It is also important to know what rights the company has for using a person's DNA. Will they run more tests when new techniques are developed? Does the test taker have to give permission or pay another fee?

Most people do not think of these scenarios before they submit a DNA sample for genealogical testing, but once a DNA test is conducted, test takers give up some control over their personal information. DNA collected as part of a medical procedure is protected by law under the Health Insurance Portability and Accountability Act (HIPAA). However, DNA collected as part of a genealogical research project is not offered the same protection. It is important for test takers to know who controls access to the database in which their DNA sequences are stored and who can override the protections that keep someone's genetic information private. Storing a DNA sequence in a database is a little like using social media. Any online database is vulnerable to infiltration by unknown entities that might wish to misuse the data stored within. Even if information is deleted in the future, someone who knows how to do so may be able to retrieve it.

Moving Past Limitations

Many people have now taken one or more DNA tests for genealogical purposes. However, these test takers still represent a tiny percentage of the entire Earth's population. As more people have their DNA tested, the genetic genealogy testing companies'

SCI-FI TO REALITY?

Science fiction authors and filmmakers are in the business of imagining how technology might be used the future, what the unintended consequences of these technologies might be, and how they might be misused. The short tandem repeat, GATTACA, occurs about 697,000 times throughout the human genome. It is also the title of a 1997 science fiction film. This film explores the concepts of genetic discrimination and eugenics. Eugenics is the idea that the human race could be improved by allowing only certain people, those with so-called desirable traits, to have children. In the film, the main character is born outside the approved eugenics program and has been labeled an "invalid." In order to join the space program, he is forced to steal the genetic code of a "valid." While the film is an action-adventure roller coaster and fun to watch, it also raises an important question: who gets to decide what is "valid" and what is not?

Gattaca questions the morality of genetically manipulating offspring to ensure the inheritance of desirable traits.

databases will grow in size and so will the power of genetic genealogy. In the meantime, test takers should understand that the reference populations their DNA sequences are compared to are not evenly distributed throughout all ethnic groups.

Even as DNA testing becomes more commonplace and more accurate, it is unlikely that it will replace traditional genealogical research. Most people who dig into their ancestries are looking for things that are personal and tangible—the yellowed, historical announcement of an ancestor's birth or marriage, for example, or a newly found family photograph. Holding these types of documents give people a sense of connection to their past that DNA analysis is unlikely to replace. However, where the twists and turns of history have obscured these personal histories or destroyed these documents, DNA testing can offer some answers that can connect people to their families' pasts.

DNA testing should be considered just another tool in the genealogist's toolbox. While it can certainly be a powerful tool, it will not answer all questions, just as census records, birth records, deeds, and other historical documents alone cannot provide all the answers to genealogical questions. However, used in conjunction with genealogical documentation, photographs, a family's oral traditions, and other materials, DNA testing can help confirm or correct family trees and pedigrees. This mix of evidence can be much more illuminating than any one type can provide in isolation.

Before embarking on a genetic genealogy quest, much thought should be given to the ethics and application of both individual DNA results and the information it reveals about other people in the family. While discovering your family history through DNA can be extremely interesting, it does have the potential to be disruptive. Taking the chance on finding biological truths about

When used alongside traditional genealogical evidence, such as census records, birth and death certificates, and old family photographs, DNA testing can be a powerful tool for filling in a family tree.

yourself is an individual choice. However, a DNA test does not only reveal your history. It also reveals the genetic history of quite a few other people and its results may have wider implications. The best way to make sure you are prepared to face any unintended consequences of the procedure is to educate yourself thoroughly and then proceed with caution.

Bibliography

"All About the Human Genome Project (HGP)." National Human Genome Research Institute. Retrieved October 26, 2017. https://www.genome.gov/10001772/all-about-the-human-genome-project-hgp/.

Belluz, Julia. "Genetic Testing Brings Families Together—and Sometimes Tears Them Apart." *Vox*, December 18, 2014. Retrieved 18 July 2017. https://www.vox.com/2014/9/9/6107039/23andme-ancestry-dna-testing.

Bettinger, Blaine T. *The Family Tree Guide to DNA Testing and Genetic Genealogy*. Cincinnati, OH: Family Tree Books, 2016.

"Career Profiles: Genealogist." National Human Genome Research Institute. Retrieved October 24, 2017. https://www.genome.gov/genomiccareers/career.cfm?id=17.

Dowell, David R. *NextGen Genealogy: The DNA Connection*. Santa Barbara, CA: Libraries Unlimited, 2015.

Gates Jr., Henry Louis. *Finding Your Roots: The Official Companion to the PBS Series*. Chapel Hill, NC: The University of North Carolina Press, 2014.

Howell, Catherine Herbert, with K. David Harrison. *People of the World: Cultures and Traditions, Ancestry and Identity*. Washington, DC: National Geographic, 2016.

International Society of Genetic Genealogy Wiki. "Genetic Genealogy Resources." Retrieved October 26, 2017. https://isogg.org/wiki/Wiki_Welcome_Page.

Jakman, Alan. "Forensic Genealogy—The Real Story." *Forensic Magazine*, December 6, 2016. Retrieved October 25, 2017. https://www.forensicmag.com/article/2016/12/forensic-genealogy-real-story.

Jestes, Roberta. "STRs vs SNPs, Multiple DNA Personalities." DNAeXplained, February 10, 2014. Retrieved October 26, 2017. https://dna-explained.com/2014/02/10/strs-vs-snps-multiple-dna-personalities/.

Jones, Nancy Lee, and Amanda K. Sarata. "Genetic Information: Legal Issues Relating to Discrimination and Privacy." Congressional Research Service. Retrieved October 13, 2017. https://biotech.law.lsu.edu/crs/rl30006_20080310.pdf.

Maldarelli, Claire. "Could Having Your DNA Tested Land You in Court?" *Popular Science*, October 16, 2015. Retrieved October 25, 2017. https://www.popsci.com/could-submitting-your-dna-to-private-genetics-companies-land-you-in-court.

"Map of Human Migration." *National Geographic.* Retrieved October 13, 2017. https://genographic.nationalgeographic.com/human-journey.

Rodriguez, Gregory. "How Genealogy Became Almost as Popular as Porn." *Time,* May 30, 2014. Retrieved October 13, 2017. http://time.com/133811/how-genealogy-became-almost-as-popular-as-porn/.

Smith, Dinitia, and Nicholas Wade. "DNA Test Finds Evidence of Jefferson Child by Slave." *New York Times*, November 1, 1998. Retrieved October 24, 2017. http://www.nytimes.com/1998/11/01/us/dna-test-finds-evidence-of-jefferson-child-by-slave.html.

Sykes, Bryan. *DNA USA: A Genetic Portrait of America*. New York, NY: Liveright Publishing, 2012.

Glossary

admixture Characteristic DNA signatures that link a group of people with mixed ancestry.

alleles Alternate forms of a gene that arise due to mutation and that reside at the same location on homologous chromosomes.

autosome Any chromosome that is not a sex chromosome.

chromosomes Microscopic structures that contain DNA and are passed down from parent to child.

crossing over The exchange of genetic material between two homologous chromosomes.

DNA (deoxyribonucleic acid) The chemical compound that contains instructions for building proteins.

dominant inheritance A mode of inheritance in which a person expresses a trait if he or she inherits just one copy of the gene.

ethnicity A social group that shares a common national or cultural tradition.

eugenics A philosophy that argues for controlled breeding in order to increase desirable traits in the human population.

gamete A sperm or egg cell.

gene A sequence of DNA bases that provides instructions for making a protein.

homologous chromosomes A pair of chromosomes with the same structure and pattern of genes, one inherited from the father and the other passed down by the mother.

marker A specific DNA sequence with a known location in the genome.

mitochondria Organelles in the cytoplasm of most cells that contain their own independent genome.

mutation A change in the sequence of DNA nucleotides.

nucleotide The four chemicals that make up the DNA code: adenine, cytosine, guanine, thymine.

reference population A group of people with which an individual's DNA is compare to in hopes of finding matching segments, indicating a shared ancestry.

short tandem repeat (STR) A pattern of two or more nucleotides repeated adjacent to each other.

single nucleotide polymorphism (SNP) A difference in a single nucleotide between two homologous chromosomes or between the genomes of two individuals.

Further Reading

Books

Chen, Jenny J. *DNA and RNA*. New York, NY: Cavendish Square, 2016.

Gerdes, Louise I. *Human Genetics*. Farmington Hills, MI: Greenhaven Press, 2014.

Jackson, Tom. *Genetics: Why We Are Who We Are*. New York, NY: Cavendish Square, 2017.

Lew, Kristi. *Understanding the Human Genome*. New York, NY: Enslow Publishing, 2018.

Lokere, Jillian. *Genetics: Unlocking the Secrets of Life*. North Mankato, MN: Essential Library, 2015.

Rutherford, Adam. *A Brief History of Everyone Who Ever Lived: The Human Story Retold Through Our Genes*. New York, NY: The Experiment, 2017.

Websites

The Genographic Project by National Geographic
genographic.nationalgeographic.com
This website explains the objectives and history of the Genographic Project, including its findings and the science behind tracing human migration using genetic information.

The International Society of Genetic Genealogy (ISOGG)
www.isogg.org
The ISOGG maintains an award-winning Wiki that describes the ins and outs of genetic genealogy, dispels myths related to the practice, and explains the science behind the different DNA tests.

Understanding the Human Genome Project
www.genome.gov/25019879/online-education-kit-understanding-the-human-genome-project
This online educational kit includes a time line of genetic discoveries and computer-animated videos that explain the structure of DNA, how it is sequenced, and how genetic variation is used to compare populations.

Index